THIS NOTEBOOK BELONGS TO:

Made in the USA
Monee, IL
18 December 2021

86363251R00056